Termite

Karen Hartley, Chris Macro, and Philip Taylor

Heinemann Library
Chicago, Illinois

Customer Service 888-454-2279
Visit our website at www.heinemannraintree.com

Designed by Ron Kamen, Michelle Lisseter, and Bridge Creative Services Limited
Illustrations by Alan Fraser at Pennant Illustration
Printed in China by South China Printing Company

10
10 9 8 7 6 5 4 3 2

New edition ISBN: 1-4034-8302-7 (hardcover)   978-1-4034-8302-7 (hardcover)
                 1-4034-8315-9 (paperback)   978-1-4034-8315-7 (paperback)

The Library of Congress has cataloged the first edition as follows:
Hartley, Karen, 1949-
        Termite / Karen Hartley, Chris Macro, and Philip Taylor.
            p. cm. -- (Bug books)
        Includes bibliographical references and index.
        Summary: A simple introduction to the physical characteristics, diet, life cycle, predators,
                habitat, and lifespan of termites.
        ISBN 1-57572-800-1 (lib. bdg.)
        1. Termites—Juvenile literature. [1. Termites.] I. Macro, Chris, 1940-. II. Taylor, Philip,
        1949-. III. Title. IV. Series.
        QL529.H28 1999
        595.7'36—dc21   98-42672
                             CIP
                             AC

Acknowledgments
The author and publishers are grateful to the following for permission to reproduce photographs:
Ardea: I Beames p. 24, H Dossenbach pp. 4, 8, 10, 15, P Goetgheluck p. 20, P Steyn p. 25,
A Warren p. 19; Bruce Coleman Ltd: G Bingham pp. 18, 29, J Burton p. 23, G Cubitt pp. 16, 26,
K Taylor pp. 6, 13, 28; FLPA: B B Casals p. 14, N Cattlin p. 9; NHPA: A Bannister p. 11; Okapia:
A Root p. 22, Dr F Sauer p. 27; Oxford Scientific Films: M Coe p. 7, S Morris p. 12,
Photolibrary.com p. 17, P Murray p. 5, A Root p. 21; Premaphotos: K Preston-Mafham p. 20.

Cover photograph reproduced with permission of NHPA/A Bannister.

The publishers would like to thank Nancy Harris for her assistance in the preparation of this book.

Some words are shown in bold, **like this**. You can find out what they mean by looking in the glossary.

Contents

What Are Termites?

Termites are small **insects** with soft bodies. All insects have six legs. Some termites have babies, some work, and some keep enemies away.

Some termites live inside trees. Some live in the soil. Sometimes millions of termites live together in one big nest. This is called a **termite mound**.

What Do Termites Look Like?

jaws

feeler

head

There are different types of termites in the nest. The **soldier** termites, like this one, attack enemies. They are blind. They have strong legs and jaws.

Flying termites have four wings and many eyes. They grow up to be **kings** and **queens**. They are the fathers and mothers. **Worker** termites have pale bodies. They have no eyes or ears.

worker

flying termite

When the **queen** is laying eggs her body swells up. She is as long as a man's finger. The **king** is much smaller. He is about the same size as your toe.

queen

king

soldier

worker

The **workers** are the smallest termites. They are about the size of your fingernail. The **soldier** termites are a bit bigger.

9

How Are Termites Born?

The **king** and **queen** live in a special room in the termite nest. The queen lays hundreds of eggs in an hour.

eggs

nymphs

The **worker** termites take care of the eggs. The eggs **hatch** into baby termites called **nymphs**. Nymphs cannot see. As they grow they become workers, **soldiers**, or flying termites.

11

As a **nymph** gets older its body grows longer. The flying termites begin to be able to see. Their bodies turn black and their wings grow.

As the **soldiers** grow, their heads get very big and they grow sharp claws. When the termites grow too big for their skin, a new skin is made. The old skin falls off. This is called **molting**.

What Do Termites Eat?

Some termites eat wood. If they get into houses they also eat paper and cloth. **Workers** chew the food and put it into the mouths of the other termites.

Some termites eat plants and soil.
Some eat a sort of **fungus**. They make
this inside their nest.

Which Animals Attack Termites?

Ants attack termites. This **termite mound** is being attacked by flying ants. Birds and other animals also attack termites.

The **soldier** termites try to fight the enemies. This soldier is being attacked by ants.

Where Do Termites Live?

Most termites live in Africa, Australia, and parts of America. Some live in very big mounds that they make with chunks of soil mixed with **saliva**.

Some termites make nests in trees. They
make the nests from something that
looks like cardboard. They make it from
chewed up wood and **body waste**.

How Do Termites Move?

Workers and **soldiers** often walk in groups carrying leaves and seeds back to the nest. They scurry along very quickly on their six legs.

When it is time for the flying termites to leave the nest, they all fly away together. Most of them die but some find a place to start a new nest.

How Long Do Termites Live?

The **king** and **queen** stay in the nest where they are safe. They can live for about 30 years. The **workers** and **soldiers** only live for a few months.

Most of the flying termites do not live for very long. When they leave the nest they cannot fly very high. Birds and other animals often eat the termites.

What Do Termites Do?

The **worker** termites are very busy.
They make the nest and build tunnels
inside so that it will stay cool. They
also feed the young termites.

The **king** and **queen** stay in their special room. When the queen is laying eggs she is so big that she cannot move. It is the **soldiers'** job to guard the entrance to the nest.

How Are Termites Special?

Worker termites are deaf and blind, but they can find their way back to the nest. When they go out they leave a trail and they smell this trail when they are coming home.

Termites can tell when other termites are near. If they are frightened they tap their heads on the ground. Termites can feel the ground move when other termites tap.

Thinking About Termites

What do you think
these termites eat?
How do you think
they made the nest?
Which kind of
termite would have
built the nest?

nest

This is a **soldier** termite.

Can you guess why it has big jaws?

What important job does the soldier do?

Bug Map

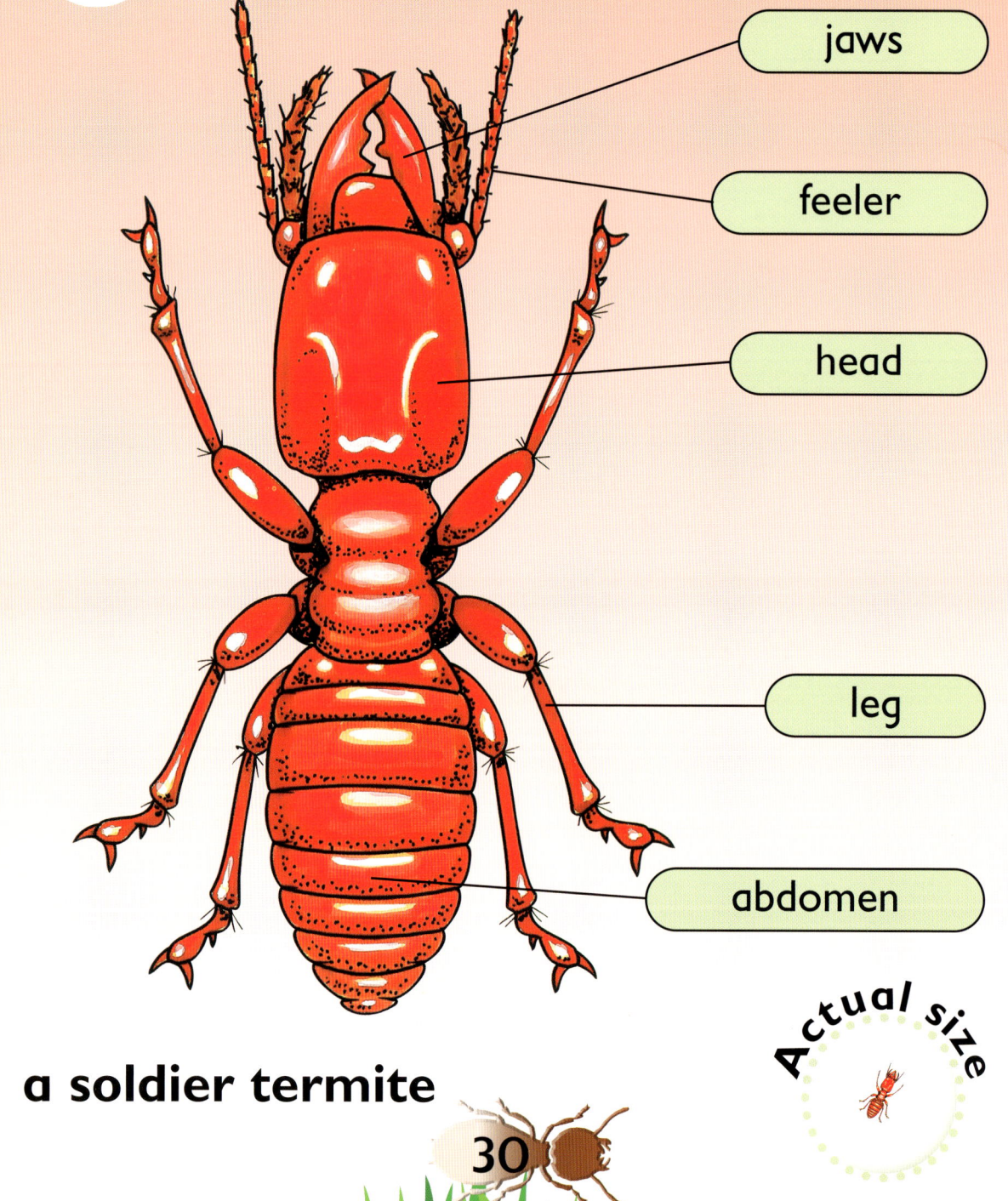

jaws

feeler

head

leg

abdomen

a soldier termite

Actual size

Glossary

body waste unwanted food that your body gets rid of when you go to the bathroom

fungus type of mould that grows in the termites' nest. The termites make it with their bodies.

hatch to come out of an egg

insect small animal with six legs

king father termite

molting when an insect grows too big for its skin it grows a new one and the old one falls off

nymph baby termite

queen mother termite that lays the eggs

saliva this is like the spit that is in your mouth

soldier termite that attacks enemies and guards the nest

termite mound very big nest that termites make above the ground. They make it with chewed up grass, chunks of soil, and saliva.

worker small termite that does all the work

Index

More Books to Read

Claybourne, Anna. *Ants and Termites.* Conn.: Franklin Watts, 2004.